Sport Climber's Guide
To Skyline Boulevard

Updated & Expanded Edition

Featuring

Castle Rock State Park,
Sanborn Skyline County Park
&
Midpeninsula Regional Open Space District
Preserves

by

Bruce Morris

MorComm Press
Palo Alto, California
1995

Sport Climber's Guide to Skyline Boulevard - First Edition.
© Bruce Morris and MorComm Press. All Rights Reserved.

Published and distributed by -

MorComm Press
443 Ventura Ave., Suite 3
Palo Alto, CA 94306-4816
Voice: (415) 856-7964
Fax: (415) 856-1719
E-mail: 72102.3167@compuserve.com

Please forward historical notes, corrections and new route information to this address.

Cover photo: Scott Cosgrove on "Oswald Cheese" (B5.11b), Klinghoffer Boulders, Castle Rock State Park, California.

All uncredited photos: Morris collection.

ACKNOWLEDGMENTS

I would like to take this opportunity to extend special thanks to all those who have contributed to a **Sport Climber's Guide to Skyline Boulevard**. Without the invaluable assistance provided by Mike Arechiga, David Caunt, Jon Hartnett, Mike Hernandez, Marc Hill, Don Simmons and Brad Watson, this project would have never been completed. Ranger Malcolm Smith of the Midpeninsula Regional Open Space District was also most helpful providing information on the local geology.

In Memoriam

John 'Yabo' Yablonski, who undoubtedly would have free-soloed all the routes in this guide.

This guide is merely a collection of notes representing various opinions on the location and relative difficulty of certain climbing routes located along the crest of the California Coast Range adjacent to Skyline Boulevard (U.S. 35). *IT IS NEITHER AN INSTRUCTIONAL MANUAL NOR A SUBSTITUTE FOR THE READER'S JUDGEMENT.*

ROCK CLIMBING IS BY ITS VERY NATURE A HIGH RISK SPORT THAT CAN RESULT IN SERIOUS INJURY OR DEATH. Therefore, be warned in advance that you must exercise your own judgment on where a route goes, its difficulty, and your ability to safely protect yourself from the intrinsic risks associated with rock climbing. It is understood that the user of this book assumes full responsibility for his or her own safety.

TABLE OF CONTENTS

MAPS

Below: Don Simmons on "Chimps In Negligée" (5.9+), Last Temptation Cliff, Castle Rock State Park, California

Chapter 1

INTRODUCTION

COAST RANGE SANDSTONE

The present volume's popular predecessor chronicled the many new short top ropes and lead climbs that had proliferated in the vicinity of Castle Rock State Park prior to 1992. Since then though several other noteworthy sandstone outcroppings have been discovered outside the geographical boundaries observed in that earlier guide. The present volume is therefore both an update to a **Sport Climber's Guide to the Castle Rock Area** (Caunt & Morris, 1992), as well as an expanded record of route activity to the north in **Aquarian Valley, Devil's Canyon** and **Eagle Peak.** Like **Summit, Indian** and **Castle Rocks**, all these previously undocumented areas are located a short distance, either east or west, of Skyline Boulevard (U.S. 35) as it meanders along the crest of the Coast Range between Page Mill Road in the north and U.S. 17 in the south (See **Map 1** and **Map 4**).

Most of the rocks in this section of the Northern California Coast Range are composed of erosion sculpted sandstone that formed the bottom of an ancient ocean some twenty-five million years ago. As summit ridges began to fold upwards to altitudes between 2600 and 3300 feet, the chemical action of rain water then carved this primeval sea bed into hundred of caves and roofs, creating a honeycomb structure unique to the region. This "Tafoni" process has also resulted in many pocketed faces and arêtes, some with dark brown knobs embedded in the otherwise largely yellow, gray, or red colored rock.

These characteristics of Coast Range sandstone require a wide range of climbing techniques. In the **Aquarian Valley,** for example, you can edge a delicate low-angle slab only a few feet away from a twenty-foot 5.12 roof. However, if you wish to sharpen your crack climbing skills, there is a greater concentration of Yosemite-type hand and fist jams at **Summit Rock** than at any of the other areas, most of which offer an abundance of steep faces, challenging arêtes, and intimidating overhangs.

CAUTION: **It is important to remember that Coast Range sandstone remains extremely fragile for up to three days following a typical winter rain storm.**

HOW TO USE THIS GUIDE

This guide provides topographic diagrams of over three hundred sport climbs, top-ropes, and boulder problems along Skyline Boulevard (U.S. 35) and tells you how to reach and identify them. For the first time, descriptions are also included of the older established areas around the main **Castle Rock** and **Goat Rock**. A separate chapter covers the excellent boulder problems long associated with Coast Range sandstone, which has been compared favorably to that found in the enchanted forest of Fontainebleau near Paris. Barry Bates, David Caunt, Scott Cosgrove and the late John Yablonski all refined their craft here to ankle-shattering precision.

Climbing areas are arranged by individual chapter in the same order one would encounter them driving north to south on Skyline Boulevard (U.S. 35), which is easily accessible from the main population centers of the Silicon Valley or Santa Cruz via U.S. 9. **Map 1** and **Map 4** provide overviews of northern and southern sections of the Skyline, including portions of the California Coast Range in San Mateo, Santa Clara and Santa Cruz Counties.

Learn your way along the Skyline crest by referring to these maps. Pick an area that interests you. Next, look up the corresponding chapter for more detailed instructions on the approach. Each chapter begins with a brief description of the characteristics unique to that area.

Climbing routes are assigned letters in alphabetical order, from left to right, as the cliff is viewed from the front.

Key to the Topos

50' - Height of climb in feet

$\mathbf{F}$ - Left facing corner

$\mathbf{\mathcal{F}}$ - Right facing corner

$\text{\textasteriskcentered}$ - Arete

$\text{\textdaggerdbl}$ - Straight in corner

$\pi\pi$ - Ledge

$\sqcup\sqcup$ - Overhang

● - Cave or hole

○ - Knob (unshaded)

⸭ - Line of route

× - Bolt

\ - Crack

5.11d - Difficulty where shown

RATINGS and EQUIPMENT

The Yosemite Decimal System (YDS) is employed throughout. The YDS is open-ended and has emerged as the *de facto* standard for rating the difficulty of roped climbing in North America, extending at present from 5.0 to 5.14. As originally suggested by Jim Bridwell in 1975, letter subgrades of a, b, c, and d are assigned to routes rated 5.10 or harder.

Recommended routes are also given an overall quality rating using a star system, with one star (★) assigned for above average quality; two stars (★★) for very high quality; and three stars (★★★) for extremely high quality - (i.e. an established local classic).

Appendix A grades all routes according to difficulty.

In those cases where a route takes more protection than a rack of quick draws, such additional gear requirements are noted. Since most of these routes are short (between 25 and 75 feet), those rare exceptions requiring more than one standard 165 foot rope to rappel (or top-rope) are identified.

ACCESS and PARKING

At present, free day parking is available in front of **Indian**, **Castle** and **Summit Rocks**. If you elect to use the large public parking lot behind the fence at Castle Rock State Park, remember there is a $3.00 per day user fee. This lot is the only legal place to park overnight along Skyline Boulevard (U.S. 35). Be warned that all other spots are ticketed after dusk.

Park for the **Aquarian Valley**, **Devil's Canyon**, **Eagle Peak** or **Skyline Slabs** only at the Grizzly Flat turnout for Upper Stevens Creek County Park as indicated on **Map 1**.

CAUTION: The **Tower of Pain** is on private property. If you climb on this formation, be prepared to be cited for trespassing and arrested!

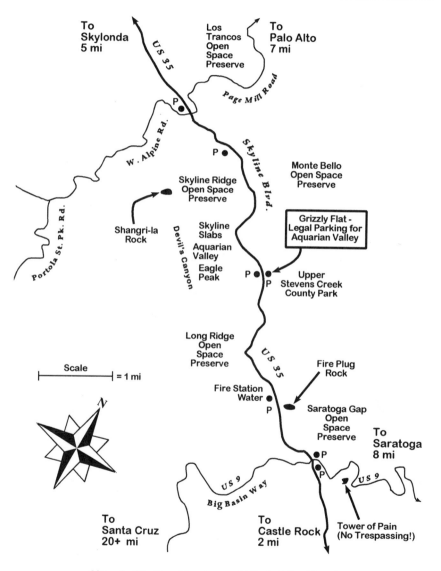

Map 1. Skyline Boulevard (U.S. 35) - North

Below: "The Claw - Center" (5.9), Eagle Peak, Long Ridge Open Space Preserve

Chapter 2

SKYLINE BOULEVARD - NORTH

Skyline Slabs, **Aquarian Valley**, **Eagle Peak** and **Devil's Canyon** are interconnected climbing areas located approximately ½ mile west of Skyline Boulevard (US 35) on **Long Ridge Open Space Preserve**. See the map on the next page (**Map 2**) to find out where to park to access these fine little crags, many of which have been utilized for roped, bolted lead climbing since at least the mid-1960s.

Midpeninsula Regional Open Space District Preserves

Some of these climbing areas lie within the present boundaries of the **Midpeninsula Regional Open Space District**, which does not officially oppose technical rock climbing here, but which does prohibit it further north in **El Corte de Madera Creek Open Space Preserve** where imposing moss-covered sandstone towers (the so-called 'Sand Caves') have been carved into a fragile lattice-work through aeolian erosion. However, what District Ordinance 93-1 does specifically prohibit in **Long Ridge Open Space Preserve** is deliberately cleaning lichen off rock with wire brushes (Section 702.1) and the placement of any new permanent fixed anchors (Section 702.3). Therefore, it is in your own long-term best interest to abide by these regulations while also maintaining *an extremely low profile whenever approaching or climbing on any of these formations.*

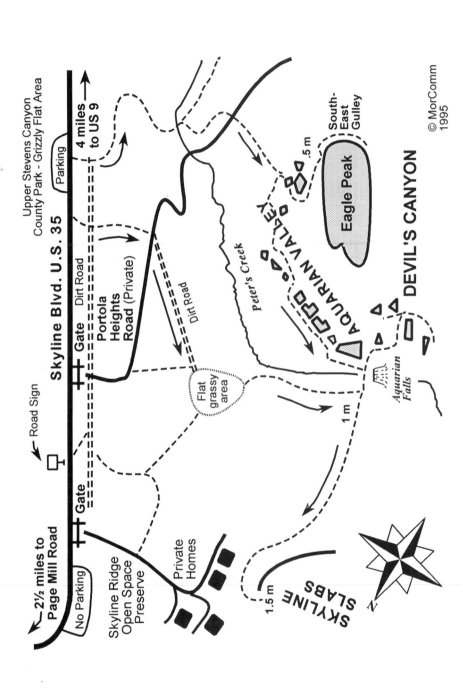

Upper Stevens Canyon
County Park - Grizzly Flat Area

Skyline Blvd. U.S. 35

4 miles → to US 9

Parking

2½ miles to Page Mill Road

No Parking

Road Sign

Gate

Gate

Dirt Road

Portola Heights Road (Private)

Dirt Road

Flat grassy area

Skyline Ridge Open Space Preserve

Private Homes

Peter's Creek

AQUARIAN VALLEY

Aquarian Falls

1 m

.5 m

South-East Gulley

Eagle Peak

DEVIL'S CANYON

SKYLINE SLABS

1.5 m

N

© MorComm 1995

Chapter 3

SKYLINE SLABS

The northwest apron of **Skyline Slabs** provides a secluded retreat to sharpen friction and low-angle face climbing skills. On the hike in take care to avoid trespassing on the property of the owner whose home sits on the ridge directly in back of the slabs.

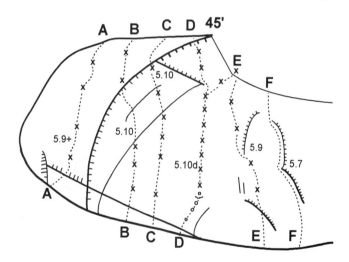

SKYLINE SLABS - NORTHWEST APRON

A   **Cranberries** 5.9+ (★)
B   **Unknown** 5.10
C   **Unknown** 5.10
D   **Old Bolt Ladder** 5.10c/d (★★)
E   **Unknown** 5.9
F   **TR** 5.7 lieback

Below: Mike Hernandez top-roping "Happy New Year" (5.10d), Devil's Canyon

Chapter 4

AQUARIAN VALLEY

Crossing *Peter's Creek* just above *Aquarian Falls* brings you to the base of the **Waterfall Wall**, first (and tallest) of the impressive sculpted sandstone towers scattered along the southwestern slopes of **Aquarian Valley**. This area acquired its cosmic nickname during the psychedelic era when tribes of colorful vagabonds inhabited the caves directly beneath the overhangs that now attract climbers to this same shady hillside with its canopy of giant madrones.

The map on the next page (**Map 3**) illustrates in detail the trails used to access this lush, secluded valley. A temperate marine climate means that the **Aquarian** is usually cooler in summer and warmer in winter than the more Sonoran regions further south around **Castle Rock State Park**.

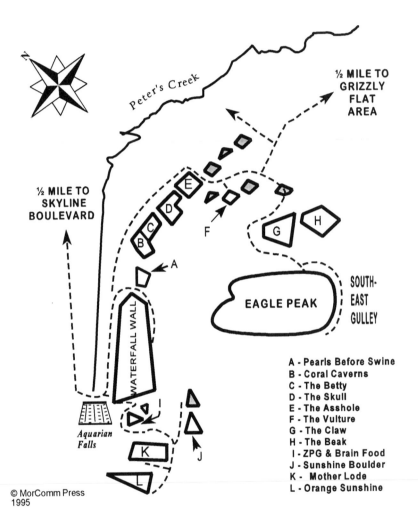

½ MILE TO
GRIZZLY
FLAT
AREA

Peter's Creek

½ MILE TO
SKYLINE
BOULEVARD

E

D

C

B

F

G

H

A

SOUTH-
EAST
GULLEY

WATERFALL WALL

EAGLE PEAK

Aquarian
Falls

I

K

J

L

A - Pearls Before Swine
B - Coral Caverns
C - The Betty
D - The Skull
E - The Asshole
F - The Vulture
G - The Claw
H - The Beak
I - ZPG & Brain Food
J - Sunshine Boulder
K - Mother Lode
L - Orange Sunshine

Map 3. Trail Map of Aquarian Valley

Waterfall Wall

A few overhangs add variety to these concentrated exercises in friction and slab climbing.

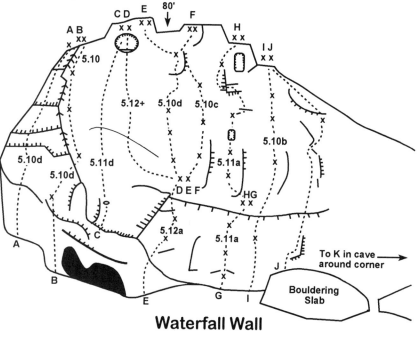

Waterfall Wall

A	**Morris Minor TR** 5.10d
B	**Morris Code** 5.10d (★★), pre-clip 1st bolt
C	**Morris Plan TR** 5.11d (★)
D	**Caunt Face TR** 5.12+
E	**Boogers** 5.10c/d (**Direct** 5.12a mantle) (★★)
F	**Green Thumb** 5.10c
G	**Isn't** 5.11a (with tree); 5.12b (without tree)
H	**S'not** 5.11a (★)
I	**Unnamed** 5.10b R
J	**TR** 5.9
K	**Stoner Cave TR** 5.12a (★)

Pearls Before Swine

This deceptively easy-looking slab route ascends the center of the small apron immediately east of the **Waterfall Wall**. A large tree on top provides an excellent natural anchor, so be sure to bring a few extra runners.

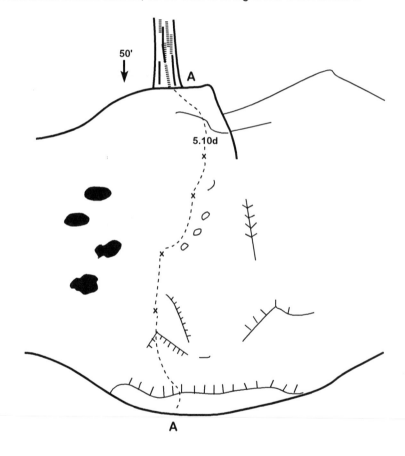

A   Pearls Before Swine 5.10d slab (★★)

Coral Caverns

These fragile overhangs are hidden behind dense foliage approximately 150 yards uphill and left from **Pearls Before Swine**.

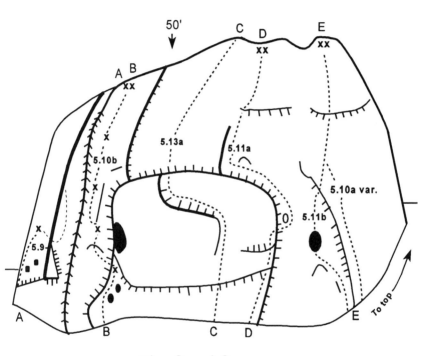

The Coral Caverns

A   **Dirty Mind** 5.9- pro: 1" to 2½"
B   **Green Room** 5.10b
C   **Cave Bitch TR** 5.13a
D   **Coral Cavern TR** 5.11a (★★)
E   **Face Bitch TR** 5.11b (★)

The Betty

This demanding little crag sits just around the corner from the **Coral Caverns**.

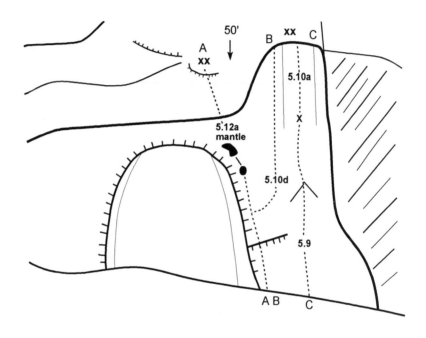

The Betty

A   **Sweaty Betty TR** 5.12a (★★)
B   **Sweaty Eddy TR** 5.10d
C   **Suicide Solution** 5.10a, pro. to 2½"

The Skull

On the west face, **"Skull & Cross-bones"** lives up to this crag's ominous name.

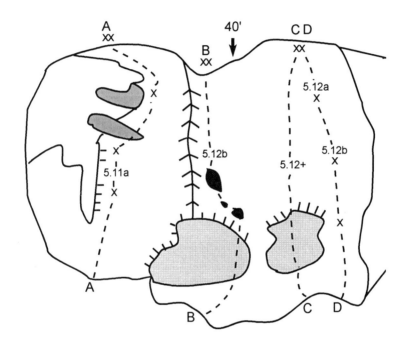

The Skull

A	Axe Blades From Hell 5.11a (★)
B	Skull F__k TR 5.12b
C	Give Me Skull TR 5.12+
D	Skull & Cross-bones 5.12b R/X (★★)

The Asshole

Huge swings off pocket-pulls characterize this impressive twenty-foot roof.

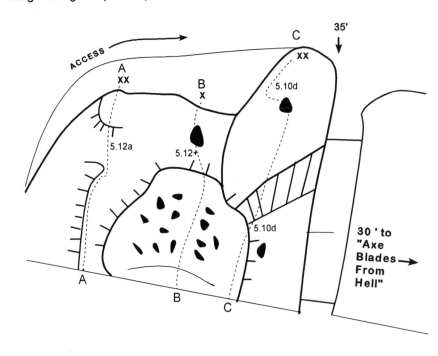

The Asshole

A   **Broken Hearts Are For Assholes, TR** 5.12a (★)
B   **The Asshole TR** 5.12+
C   **Broken Asshole TR** 5.10d (★)

Chapter 5

EAGLE PEAK

Eagle Peak, actually a massive low-angle slab, faces the Pacific across the manzanita covered hillside above the **Aquarian Valley**. To reach it, continue several hundred more yards uphill beyond the **Asshole** until the trail levels out, turn right, and descend past the **Beak** and the **Claw** to the back of the main slab proper.

Although endless possibilities for friction wandering exist here, all the more technical climbs, including an atypical dihedral crack, rise out of the brush-choked southeast gulley.

The Vulture

The best way to approach the **Vulture** formation is by descending down a deer path leading through the manzanita jungle to the top from behind.

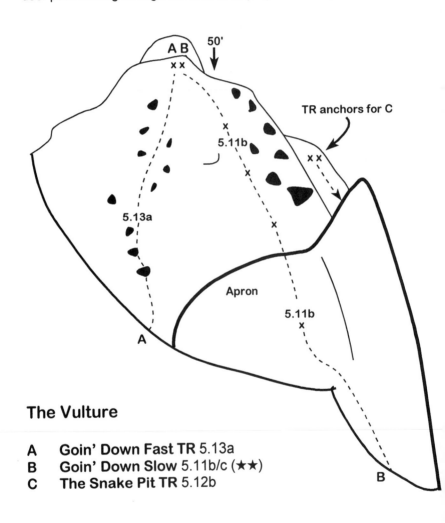

The Vulture

A	**Goin' Down Fast TR** 5.13a	
B	**Goin' Down Slow** 5.11b/c (★★)	
C	**The Snake Pit TR** 5.12b	

The Claw and The Beak

These two towers create a sheltered winter sun-bowl behind the true summit of **Eagle Peak**.

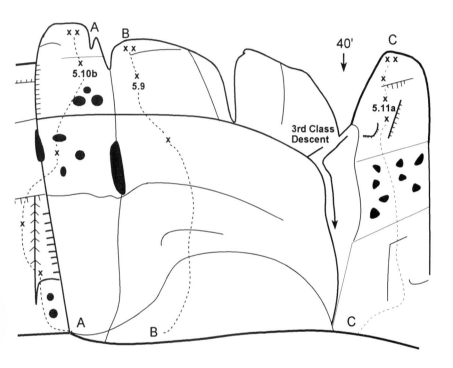

The Claw and The Beak - West Faces

A   **The Claw** - Left 5.10b
B   **The Claw** - Center 5.9
C   **The Beak** 5.11a (★)

Main Eagle Peak - Southeast Gulley

Continue on past the **Beak** and the **Claw** until it becomes possible to descend left from the backside of **Eagle Peak** into the brush-choked southeast gulley where a few technical climbs are hidden away.

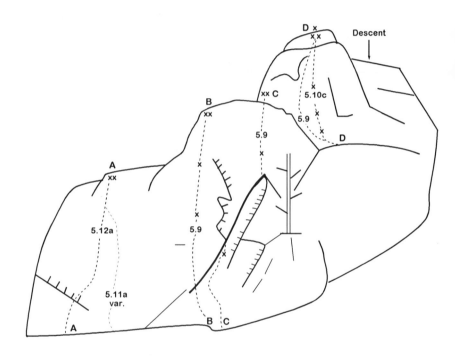

Eagle Peak - Southeast Gulley

A	Gold Wall TR 5.12a
B	Face-Corner 5.9
C	Classic Crack 5.9 (★)
D	Face 5.10c (or **TR** var. 5.9)

Chapter 6

DEVIL'S CANYON

To access the short faces and arêtes of **Devil's Canyon,** cross *Peter's Creek* just before it plunges over *Aquarian Falls*, crawl through the so-called "Stoner Cave," then descend west down an indistinct, loose trail. The first rock you will encounter is the extremely overhanging top-rope **ZPG**. Not far away, hidden in a grotto next to the falls, is a difficult twenty-foot finger crack, "The Aquarium" (5.11b). Continuing down a couple hundred yards further brings you to one of the best cliffs in the whole area, **The Mother Lode**. Descending all the way to the very bottom to visit the **Orange Sunshine Cliff** will sometimes warrant the arduous uphill trug back out, however.

ZPG (Zero Population Growth)

Safely top-roping **ZPG Now!** requires pre-clipping the directional bolt.

A   **ZPG Now! TR** 5.12b (★★)
B   **Power Mad TR** 5.12a
C   **Brain Food** 5.11a (★)
D   **The Aquarium TR** 5.11b

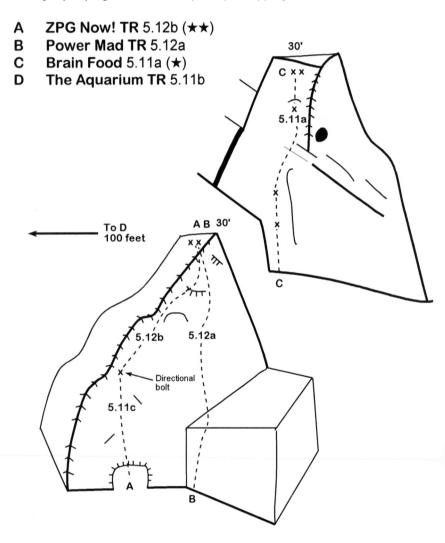

The Mother Lode

This incredible little cliff boasts several worthy routes, including a "sporty" 5.11b face and a must-do five-ten clip route.

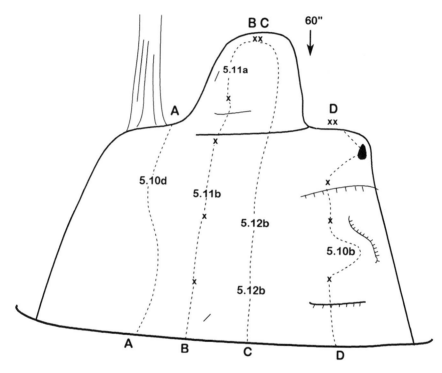

The Mother Lode

A	**Green Bud** 5.10d TR, Anchor with long slings from small tree.
B	**Mother Load** 5.11b R (★★★)
C	**Panning For Holds** 5.12b (★)
D	**Chewy's Lookout** 5.10b (★★)

The Sunshine Boulder

The continuously overhanging west face offers two challenging top-ropes.

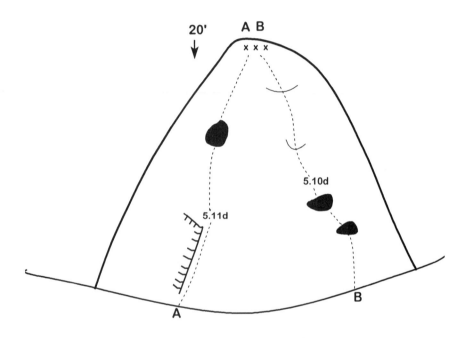

The Sunshine Boulder

A **Merry Chrismas** TR, 5.11d (★)
B **Happy New Year** TR 5.10d (★)

Orange Sunshine Cliff

This prow sits at the very bottom of **Devil's Canyon,** almost at the exact spot where local legend recalls the "Family of Love" once operated their notorious STP-LSD factory.

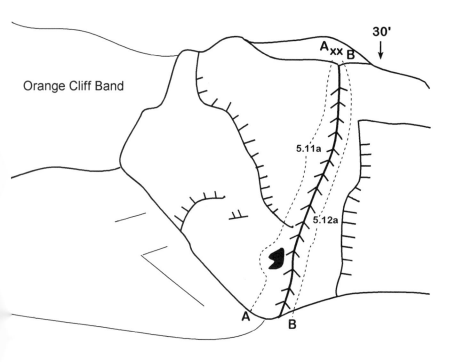

Orange Sunshine Cliff

A **Orange Barrell TR** 5.11a
B **Orange Barrel Arête TR** 5.12a

Below: Scott Cosgrove on "Oswald Cheese Direct" (B1),
Klinghoffer Boulders

Chapter 7

STEVENS CANYON BOULDER

This serpentine outcropping guards the eastern entrance to **Stevens Creek County Park** along the shortcut leading from **South Foothill Boulevard** to **U.S. 9** via **Redwood Gulch Road**. The south face overhangs Stevens Creek and provides a cool place to escape the summer heat.

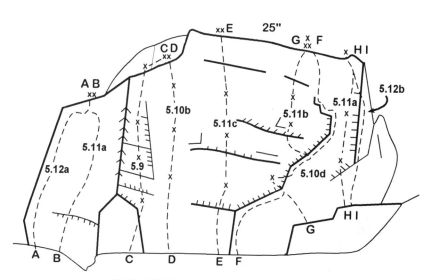

STEVENS CANYON BOULDER

A	Merciless TR 5.12a
B	Force Field TR 5.11a
C	Shit Creek 5.9
D	Shit List 510b (★)
E	Effluvia 5.11c (★★)
F	Tooth & Claw 5.10d
G	Hang Nail 5.11b
H	Fish On a Tricyle 5.11a
I	Fish On a Bicycle TR 5.12b

Below: Summit Rock (el. 3076'), Sanborn Skyline County Park, Santa Clara County, California

Chapter 8

SKYLINE BOULEVARD - SOUTH

All the most popular, established climbing areas in the Santa Cruz Mountains are located along the five-mile stretch of Skyline Boulevard (U.S. 35) south of its main intersection with U.S. 9 at Saratoga Gap. All the best bouldering rocks (including the **Parking Lot**, **Klinghoffers**, **Nature Nazis**, and **Magoos)** can be found here too. The full page road map on the next page (**Map 4**) shows where to park to access such traditional climbing areas as **Summit**, **Castle**, **Indian**, **Billy Goat** and **Goat Rocks**.

Unfortunately for climbers, the first major sandstone formation south of Saratoga Gap, **The Tower of Pain**, lies on private property where trespassing is patently illegal. In fact, if you climb here, expect to be cited by the State or County Park Rangers and, quite possibly, arrested. Topos of these routes are included here therefore for historical purposes only, since **The Tower of Pain** - like **Platypus**, **Shady Rock**, and **California Ridge** further south - also retains evidence of what must have been truly terrifying bolt-aided ascents during the late 1950s or early 1960s.

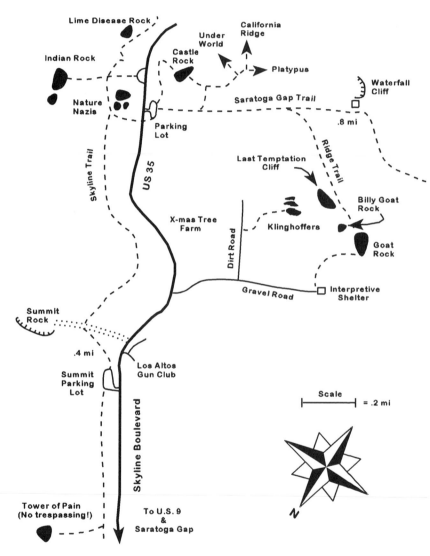

Map 4. Skyline Boulevard (U.S. 35) - South

Chapter 9

The TOWER of PAIN

This seventy-five foot sandstone spire forms a prominent landmark near the ridge line on the drive up U.S. 9 from the Silicon Valley to Saratoga Gap. **Remember: Trespassing on this rock is highly illegal!**

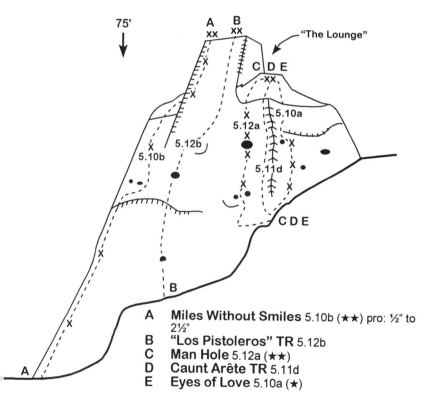

A   **Miles Without Smiles** 5.10b (★★) pro: ½" to 2½"
B   **"Los Pistoleros"** TR 5.12b
C   **Man Hole** 5.12a (★★)
D   **Caunt Arête** TR 5.11d
E   **Eyes of Love** 5.10a (★)

Tower of Pain - Northwest Face

The Tower of Pain - Southeast Face

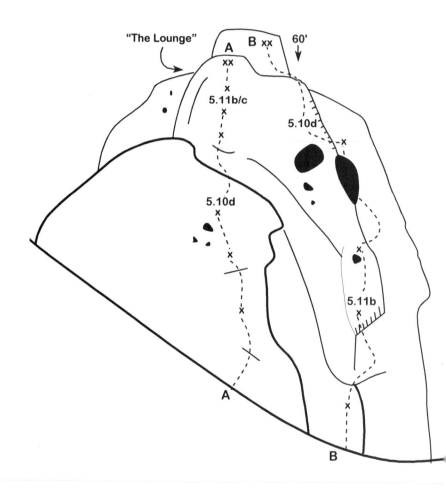

The Tower of Pain - Southeast Face

A   **The World Kills Dreamers** 5.11b/c (★)
B   **La Moulin Rouge** 5.11b (★★) pro.: include 1
         extra piece 3½" to 4" to protect the second clip.

Chapter 10

SUMMIT ROCK

The interconnected towers, cliff bands and boulders forming **Summit Rock** (el. 3,076') are located in **Sanborn Skyline County Park**, on the east side of **U.S. 35**, 1.7 miles south of the main intersection with **U.S. 9** at **Saratoga Gap (Map 4)**. Most routes ascend spectacular arêtes up to seventy-five feet in length. There are also a few Yosemite-like cracks for practicing jamming, chimney and offwidth techniques.

To get to **Summit Rock**, park at the dirt turnout on the east side of **Skyline Boulevard (U.S. 35)** just before the **Los Altos Gun Club** and walk .4 miles out a wide marked trail. When you reach the back of the main formation, a trail constructed by the Boy Scouts leads down and right, then back left, to the base of the **Lower Tier**.

NOTE: Parties that intend to climb at Summit Rock should carry
         along a plastic trash bag to carry out any glass or garbage
         they find there. Despite periodic organized clean-up days
         by volunteer groups, after dark, Summit is still being
         showered with broken glass by bottle-throwing drunks!
         Write your elected representatives to demand increased
         patrols!

SUMMIT ROCK - Upper Tier (Left)

These two crack climbs are tucked away in an alcove just off the **Boy Scout Trail** to the base of the **Lower Tier**.

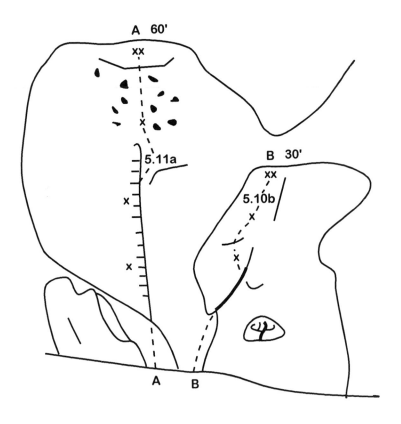

Summit Rock - Upper Tier (Left)

A   **Brain Waves 5.11a (★★)**
B   **Pogo's Nose 5.10b**, pro.: include a 2" camming device to protect the first clip.

SUMMIT ROCK - Upper Tier (Right)

The wide ledges at the base of the **Upper Tier** offer a panoramic vista of the entire Bay Area, from the Pacific Ocean to Mt. Hamilton, Mt. Diablo and beyond - often as far north as Mt. St. Helena and, sometimes, on a clear winter day, even to snow-capped Mt Lassen.

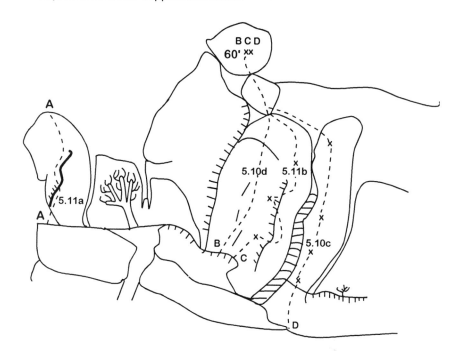

Summit Rock - Upper Tier (Right)

A **Sahib TR** 5.11a
B **Urolagniac TR** 5.10d
C **Fecolagniac** 5.11b (★★)
D **Dahmer's Delight** 5.10c (★)

SUMMIT ROCK - Lower Tier

A   Spung-Lick-A-Litus 5.12b (★★)
B   Worm Belly 5.10a
C   Unfinished Project (5.13?)
D   Ribbed For Comfort TR 5.9
E   Wide Crack 5.7
F   Bolt Filcher 5.10d (★★★)
G   U. Santa Clara Practice Climb #1 5.8
H   Double Cracks 5.9 (★), pro: 1" to 3"
I   Rectalphobiac 5.11b (★★★)
J   Glob of Shit 5.10c
K   Hand Crack/Roof 5.9, pro: medium to 3"
L   Chancroid 5.11c
M   Skill Saw Gourmet 5.11d (★★★), pro: include one
     extra piece, 2" to 2½", for hand crack below anchors.
N   U. Santa Clara Practice Climb #2 5.7
O   Tree Surgeon 5.9+ (★), pro: small to 3½"
P   Rigormorris 5.12a (★★), pro: small to medium (for
     Tree Surgeon crack start)

SUMMIT ROCK - Lower Tier

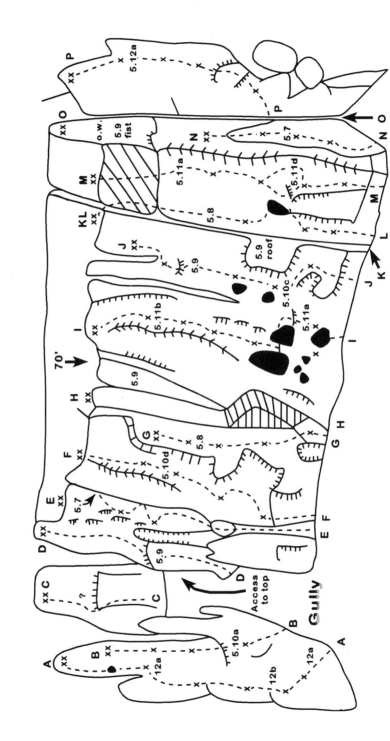

SUMMIT ROCK - Lower Tier (Far Left)

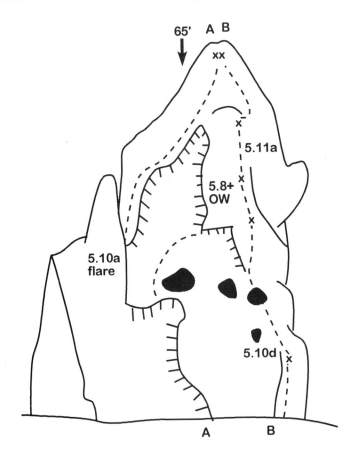

Summit Rock - Lower Tier (Far Left)

A   **Root Canal** 5.8 OW or 5.10a flare, pro: 1 to 3½"
B   **The Molar** 5.11a (★★)

SUMMIT ROCK - Lower Tier (Far Right)

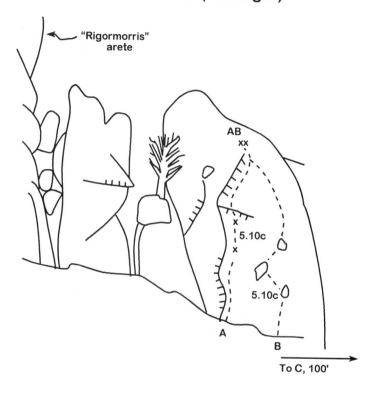

Summit Rock - Lower Tier (Far Right)

A   Peewee's Big Adventure 5.10c (★)
B   Peewee's Weewee TR 5.10c
C   Light In The Basement 5.11a (★)

SUMMIT ROCK - Outrigger Boulders

The Outriggers are a separate group of short towers located about one hundred yards downhill and left (East) from the base of the Lower Tier.

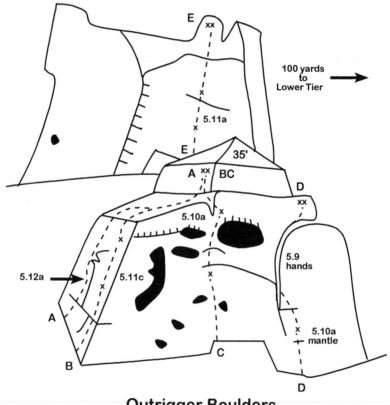

Outrigger Boulders

A   **TR** 5.12a
B   **Little Squirt** 5.11c (★★)
C   **Doughnuts With Buddha** 5.10a (★)
D   **Flare Up** 5.10a, pro: small to 3½"
E   **Little Shit** 5.11a slab

Chapter 11

INDIAN ROCK

The convoluted red sandstone towers, arêtes and caves of **Indian Rock** are located in **Sanborn Skyline County Park**, only a short walk south down Skyline Boulevard (U.S. 35) from the parking lot for **Castle Rock State Park**. Limited parking is also available directly in front of the main entrance to **Sanborn Skyline County Park**.

CASTLE ROCK STATE PARK

SANBORN SKYLINE COUNTY PARK

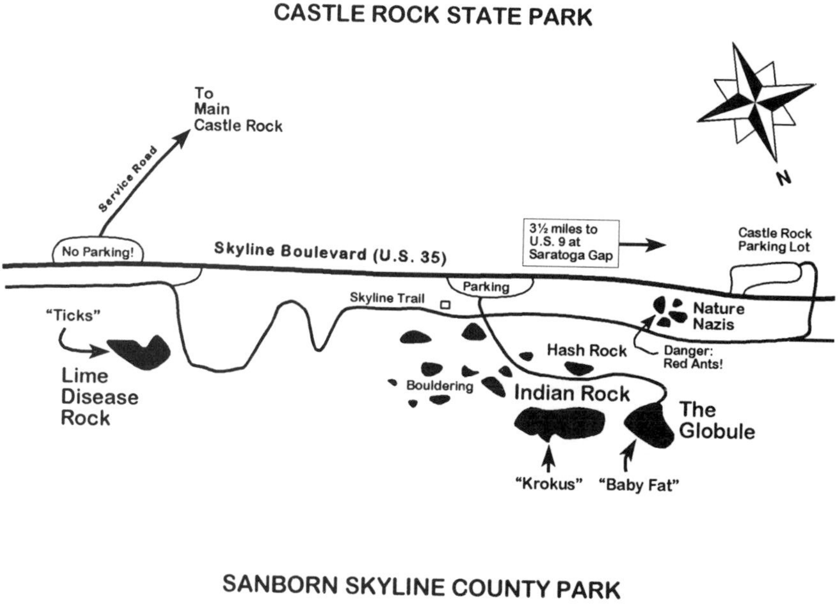

Map 5. Indian Rock Trail Map

Below: David Caunt on the first ascent of "Krokus" (5.11d), Indian Rock - North Face

INDIAN ROCK - South Face

Be sure to sample the excellent bouldering on **Hash Rock**, the little red boulder in front of this side of **Indian**.

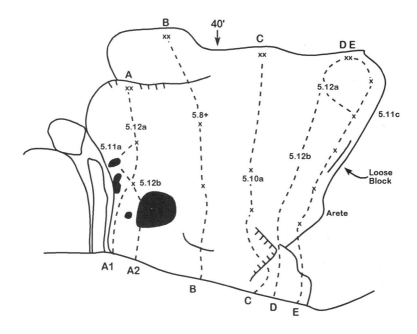

Indian Rock - South Face

A **Jail Bird** left var. 5.12a, or right var. 5.12b (★★)
B **South Face** 5.8+
C **Puckered Starfish** 5.10a (★)
D **Well Endowed TR** 5.12b
E **Donkey Dong** 5.12a or 5.11c (★★★)

INDIAN ROCK - North Face

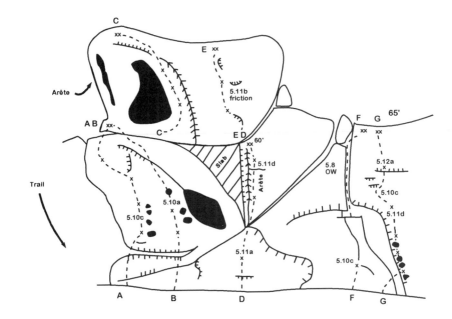

INDIAN ROCK - North Face

A   **Viscious Circles** 5.10c (★)
B   **Blowing Bubbles** 5.10a (★)
C   **Dismal Abysmal** 5.11c (★)
D   **Krokus** 5.11d (★★★), pro: include pieces in the 3" to 3½" range to protect the second clip.
E   **Hocus** 5.11b R (★)
F   **Cum Slot** 5.10c, pro: small to 3½"
G   **Strip Poker** 5.12a (★★)

The Globule

The "Fatty" Globule is a separate tower just right of the north face of **Indian Rock**.

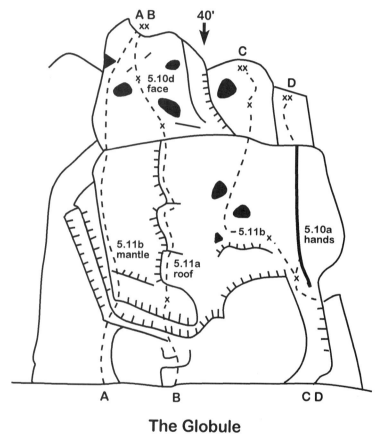

The Globule

- **A** **Mike's Donut TR** 5.11b
- **B** **Baby Fat** 5.11a (★★)
- **C** **Belly Button** 5.11b
- **D** **Jelly Belly** 5.10a (★), pro: include a few extra pieces in the ¾" to 2" range

Lime Disease Rock

To reach this secluded rock, pass through the main entrance to Sanborn Skyline Country Park, turn right down the Skyline Ridge Trail, and continue walking several hundred yards further south. The rock itself juts out from the trail like a narrow peninsula.

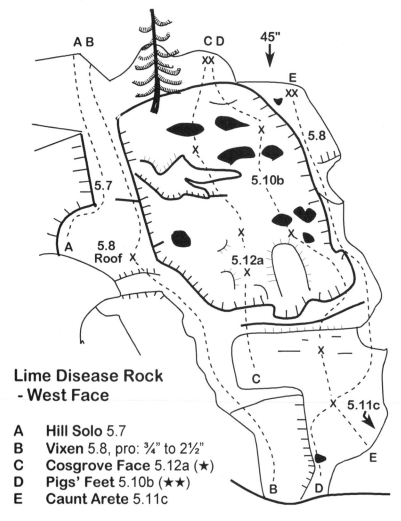

Lime Disease Rock
- West Face

A   Hill Solo 5.7
B   Vixen 5.8, pro: ¾" to 2½"
C   Cosgrove Face 5.12a (★)
D   Pigs' Feet 5.10b (★★)
E   Caunt Arete 5.11c

Lime Disease Rock - East Face

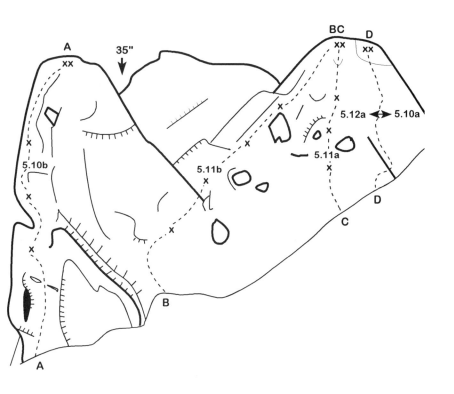

Lime Disease Rock - East Face

A **Ticks Ripped My Flesh** 5.10b (★★)
B **Unlucky In Love** 5.11b (stay on arête)
C **Lucky In Love** 5.11a mantle (★)
D **Bitch Goddess TR** 5.10a - 5.12a

Chapter 12

CASTLE ROCK

Situated in a beautiful rolling woodland some three thousand feet above the teeming Silicon Valley, in summer **Castle Rock** attracts boulderers and climbers (along with hoards of tourists). Although there are no modern bolt protected sport routes here, fifty-foot **Castle Rock** does boast a number of worthy top-ropes, some of which, like *"Aeronautical Engineer"* (5.11b), *"Mega Blast"* (5.10c) and *"Farewell to Arms"* (5.10a), have become established local classics. The surrounding area also contains dozens of uniquely shaped boulders, like the **Beak**, the **Spoon**, and the **Magoos**, all within a few minutes walk of the main south face.

Left: **Mike Hernandez on "Bates Eliminate" (B1), Magoo Boulders, Main Castle Rock Area**

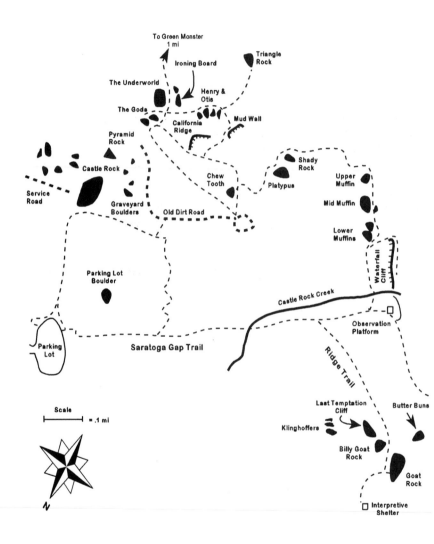

Map 6. Climber Trails Around Castle Rock Area

Castle Rock - East Face

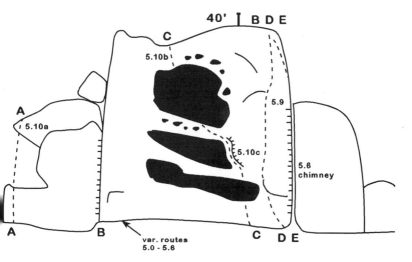

Castle Rock - East Face

- **A** Roof TR 5.10a (★)
- **B** Summit Route 5.4
- **C** Mantle Groove TR 5.10c
- **D** Face TR 5.9 (★)
- **E** Chimney TR 5.6

Castle Rock - West Face

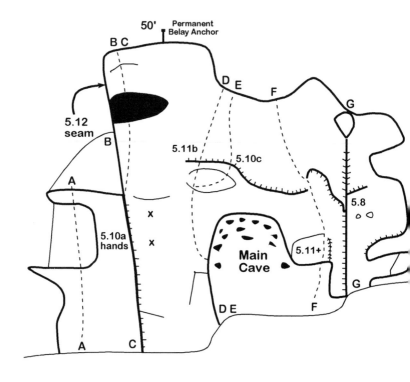

Castle Rock - West Face

- **A** Roof TR 5.10a
- **B** Overhanging Seam TR 5.12
- **C** Farewell to Arms TR 5.10a (★★)
- **D** Aeronautical Engineer TR 5.11b (★★★)
- **E** Mega Blast TR 5.10c (★)
- **F** Roof TR 5.11+
- **G** Chockstone TR 5.8

Pyramid Rock

For years, a near perfect fingers-to-hands crack has lured climbers to the secluded **Pyramid Rock,** which is located a couple hundred yards downhill southwest from its nearest neighbor, the main **Castle Rock**. The backside provides easier top-rope possibilities.

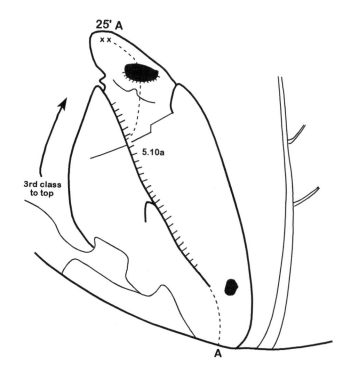

Pyramid Rock - North Face

A   Pyramid Crack TR 5.10a (★)

Chapter 13

WESTERN ADDITION

The **Western Addition** contains several small crags including the **Chew Tooth, California Ridge, Platypus**, and **Shady Rock**. All these formations are situated a few hundred yards from one another on top of a rounded hill approximately one quarter mile west of the main Castle Rock.

Left: Al "Dude" Swanson on "Plat-A-Pussy" (5.10a), The
           Platypus, Western Addition

Chew Tooth

One of the first rocks in the area to undergo extensive development (c. 1990), this fine little crag, named for its propensity for eatting ropes, still remains among the most popular.

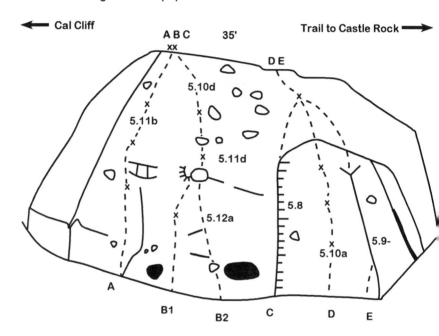

Chew Tooth - East Face

A **Left** 5.11b
B **Center B1:** 5.11d mantle or **B2:** 5.12a dyno (★★)
C **Hand Crack** 5.8, pro: 1" to 3"
D **Uncle Fred's Vacation Plan** 5.10a, after 5.11a boulder move start (★)
E **Thin Crack** 5.9-, mandatory solo

California Ridge

The flat top of what is often called **"Cal Cliff"** provides a sweeping panorama of Big Basin, the Pacific Ocean and Monterey Bay. The giant scrubbed face at the bottom of the canyon is the **Green Monster**.

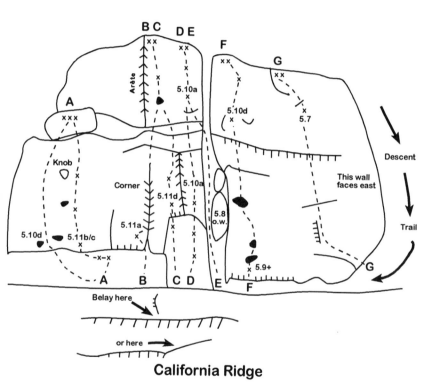

California Ridge

A	**California Five-Eleven A** 5.11b (★★★)
B	**Access Denied** 5.11a (★), pro: stoppers and camming devices ½" to 2"
C	**Ayatollah** 5.11d
D	**Mullah** 5.10a (★★)
E	**Case Dismissed** 5.10a, pro: small to 3"
F	**Guilty As Charged** 5.10d (★)
G	**Band Aids On Road Rash** 5.7, pro: small to medium, ½" to 2½"

Platypus

This forty-five foot sandstone finger is a favorite winter practice spot since most of the climbs on it face either west or south. There is also a B1 boulder traverse around the entire lower circumference of the rock.

Platypus - West Face

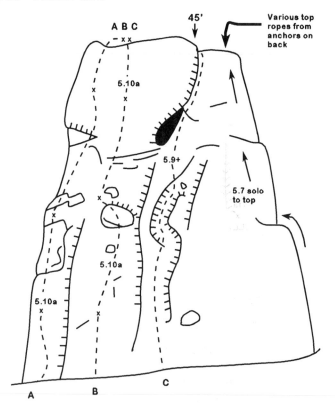

Platypus - West Face

A   **Plat-A-Pussy** 5.10a (★)
B   **Moss Man** 5.10a (★★)
C   **Howling Iguana TR** 5.9+

Platypus - North Face

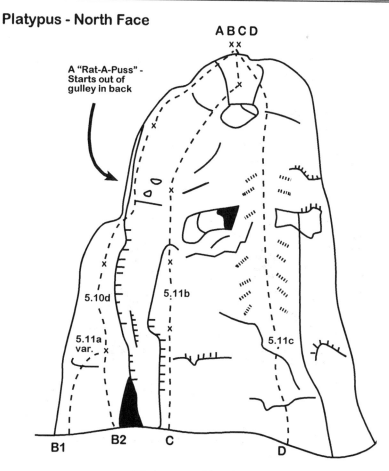

A B C D

A "Rat-A-Puss" -
Starts out of
gulley in back

5.10d

5.11b

5.11a
var.

5.11c

B1   B2   C   D

Platypus - North Face

A   **Rat-A-Puss** 5.10a (★) [around corner on backside]
B   **Al Hussein B1:** 5.11a var. or **B2:** 5.10d (★)
C   **Jelly Fish** 5.11b (★★)
D   **Embryo TR** 5.11c

Shady Rock

Hidden from prying eyes by dense foliage, the **Shady Rock** is interlaced with pockets, caves and roofs.

Shady Rock - East Face

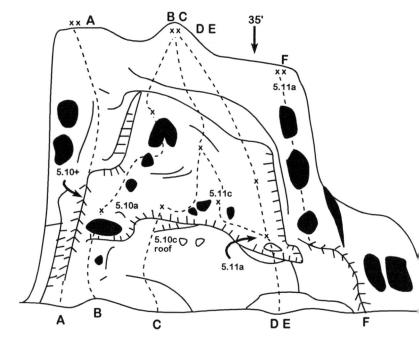

Shady Rock - East Face

A	**Thin Crack** TR 5.10+
B	**Cotton Mouth** 5.10a roof
C	**Tall Man Simplex** 5.10c roof (★)
D	**Herpes Simplex** 5.11c (★)
E	**Bad Influence** 5.11a (★)
F	**TR** 5.11a mantle

Shady Rock - West Face

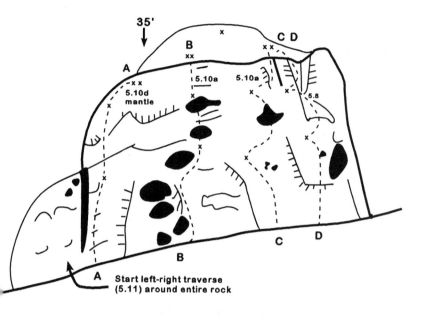

Shady Rock - West Face

A   Small Man Complex 5.10d (★)
B   Dog Breath 5.10a (★)
C   Special Effects 5.10a (★)
D   Slot Nose 5.8

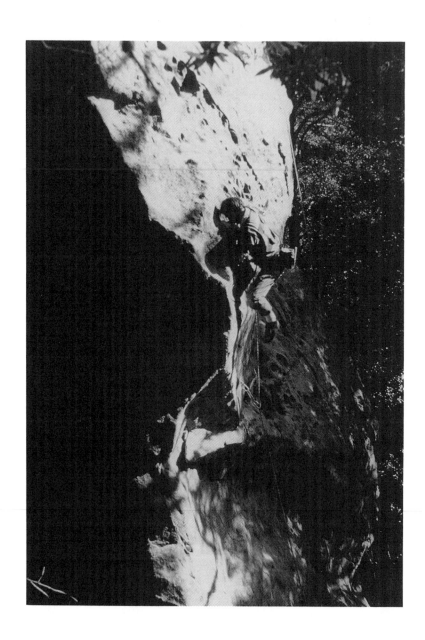

Chapter 14

The UNDERWORLD

A hundred yards before the **Chew Tooth** where the climber's trail divides, the right-hand path leads upward to the **Western Addition** and the left-hand path leads down into the dark, tree-filled valley known as the **Underworld**.

To access the many fine, moderate routes found in the **Underworld**, choose the left-hand path. After descending down it three hundred vertical feet in about a quarter mile, you will come to the back of the **Gods** formation.

Left: "Drug Lord" (5.10c), Underworld Rock

The Gods

Four, steep "two-bolt wonders" to be top-roped, led, or (self-destructive mood permitting) soloed.

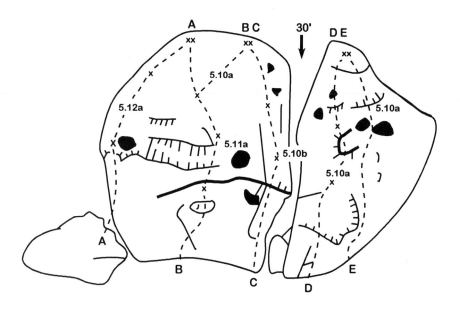

The Gods

A   Set 5.12a R
B   Cerberus 5.11a (★)
C   Anubis 5.10b (★)
D   Thoth 5.10a (★)
E   Son of Thoth TR 5.10a

Underworld Rock

At almost eight feet, the **Underworld Rock** has some of the longest moderate routes in the immediate area.

Underworld Rock - Southeast Face

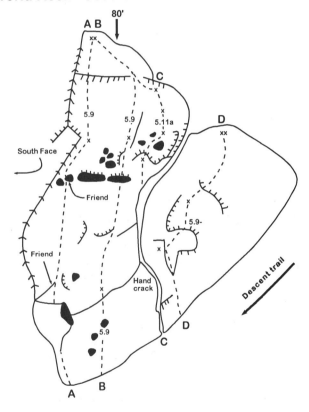

Underworld Rock - Southeast Face

A   **Hair Dresser** 5.9
B   **Balance Sheet** 5.9
C   **Underpass** 5.11a roof (★★) , pro: 1½" to 3"
D   **High On Life** 5.9- (★)

Underworld Rock - Southwest Face

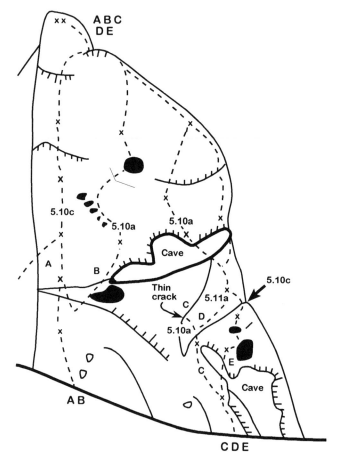

Underworld Rock - Southwest Face

A   **Drug Lord** 5.10c, or 5.11a arête start (★)
B   **Hit Man** 5.10a (★)
C   **Butt Hole Bypass** 5.10d
D   **Poop Shoot Direct** 5.11a
E   **Poop Shoot** 5.10c (★★)

Underworld Rock - West Face

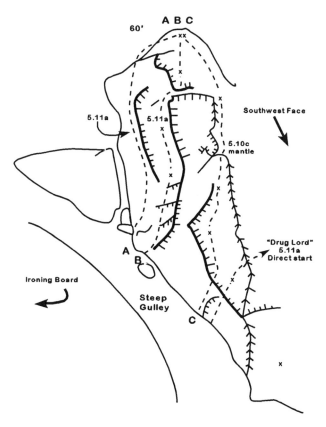

Underworld Rock - West Face

A   Lefthand Arête TR 5.11a
B   Black Market Babies 5.11a (★★)
C   Gestapo Priest 5.10c (★)

Ironing Board

The **Ironing Board** is the flat-topped formation that stands directly across the descent gulley west of **Underworld Rock**.

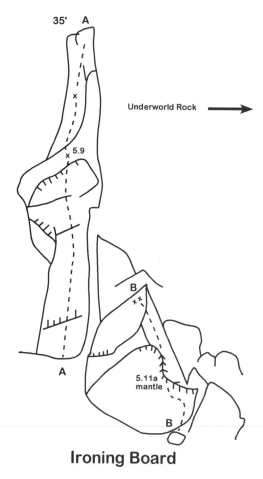

Ironing Board

A   **Ironing Board** 5.9, pro: ¼" to ¾"
B   **The Wanker** TR 5.11a

Henry & Otis Boulders

Named in honor of the anti-hero protagonists of that fine motion picture, *"Henry: Portrait of a Psycho Killer"* (1991), these four short arêtes offer some challenging top-rope diversions.

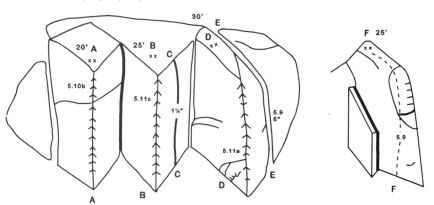

Henry & Otis Boulders

A   **Psycho Killer TR** 5.10b
B   **Otis TR** 5.11c (★★)
C   **Thin Hands Crack TR** 5.9
D   **Henry TR** 5.11a (★)
E   **Uncle Adolf** 5.9 OW
F   **Chester the Molester TR** 5.9

Mud Wall

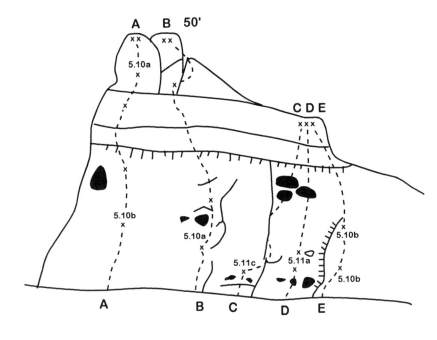

Mud Wall

A   **Mommy's Boy** 5.10b (★)
B   **Mud Pies** 5.10a
C   **Mud Crack** 5.11c/d (★), pro: ½" to 2"
D   **Mud Hole** 5.11a (★★), pro: include ¾" TCU
E   **Mud Shark** 5.10b

Triangle Rock

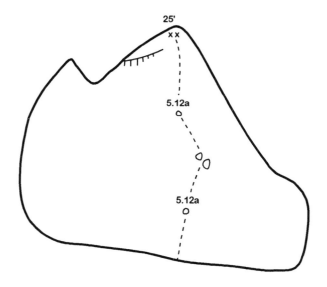

Triangle Rock

A   **Connect the Dots TR** 5.12b

Chapter 15

The GREEN MONSTER

For a rugged adventure, try taking an extended day trip to the **Green Monster**, the vegetated 120 foot cliff easily visible over a thousand feet below from the top of **California Ridge**. Start at the dry stream bed at the base of **Underworld Rock** and follow a steep trail a mile down valley until you come to a broad expanse of sculpted sandstone bedrock covered with ferns and watered by natural springs. From here, turn left and proceed another quarter mile uphill until your collide with the **Green Monster**. There are a number of other mysterious climbs here, too, further downstream on a giant flat-topped formation known as the **Heliport**. Despite the many new obvious lines to bag, the fourteen hundred foot uphill hike back out is certain to limit the popularity of this beautiful, isolated valley.

Caution: Although fear of Mountain Lions is usually more imaginary than real, be aware that these large cats do inhabit this remote region.

Left: Mike Arechiga on "Clamydia" (5.11d), Castle Rock Falls

Green Monster Cliff

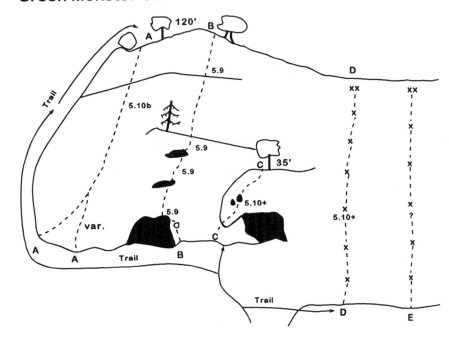

Green Monster Cliff

A   **Twin Oaks TR** 5.10b (★)
B   **Madrone Direct** 5.9 (★★), all natural pro:
5/8" to 3"; include extra runners.
C   **Roof TR** 5.10+
D   **Unnamed** 5.10d (★)
E   **Unknown** (?)

Chapter 16

CASTLE ROCK FALLS

With the notable exceptions of **Indian** and **Summit Rocks**, the **Waterfall Cliff** contains more consistently high-standard, high-quality bolted sport climbs than any other similar-sized formation in the Castle Rock region.

To get to the top of the **Waterfall Cliff**, follow the **Saratoga Gap Trail** eight tenths of a mile (.8 mi) due west from the **Castle Rock Parking Lot**. A few hundred feet after passing the fork where the **Ridge Trail** branches off right to begin the climb to **Last Temptation Cliff** and **Goat Rock**, you will come to a metal **Observation Platform** that overlooks the *Falls*.

The traditional method of accessing the popular **Falls Route** (5.8+ or 5.10a), is to rappel in and climb out from the supports at the base of this platform (two ropes required). However, the best way of approaching the majority of climbs on this cliff is to cross *Castle Rock Creek* fifty yards upstream from the viewing platform and then follow a rough trail uphill and south for about 300 hundred feet until it becomes possible to descend a leaf-filled gully leading down and right to the very base of the cliff. The first climb you will come to is the obvious 5.6 dihedral start to **"Degeneration"** (5.10a).

The Muffins

The Muffins are really oversized boulders, all about thirty-five feet in height, clustered together in a group on the oak-covered hillside that rises to the southeast behind the main **Waterfall Cliff**.

Lower Muffins - West Faces

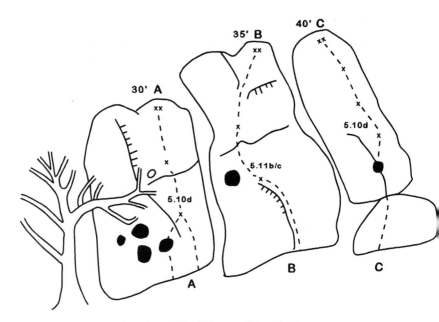

Lower Muffins - West Faces

A   **Corn Muffin** 5.10d (★)
B   **Burnt Muffin** 5.11b/c (★★)
C   **Jelly Roll** 5.10d

Mid-Muffin - West Face

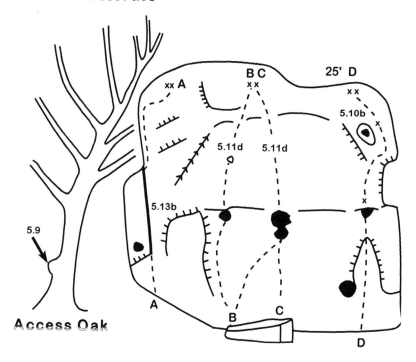

Mid-Muffin - West Face

A   **Muffin Monster TR** 5.13b (★★)
B   **Liar's Dice TR** 5.11d
C   **Body Cast TR** 5.11d (★)
D   **Muff Diver** 5.10b (★)

Waterfall Cliff - Right Side

A   **Lieback Corner** 5.7, pro: 1" to 3"
B   **Above the Law** 5.11d (★★)
C   **Clamydia** 5.11d (★★★)
D   **Dendritis TR** 5.12b
E   **Cleotitis** 5.12b (★★)
F   **Black Dragon TR** 5.11d (★)
G   **POS Crack** 5.10c, pro: small to 3½"
H   **Convulsions** 5.11b, pro: ¾" to 2" (★★)
I   **Leading To Death** 5.9 (Direct Start: 5.10d TR), pro: medium to 2½"
J   **Putrefaction** 5.11a (★★★)
K   **Degeneration** 5.10a, pro: ½" to 2½" (★★)

Waterfall Cliff - Right Side

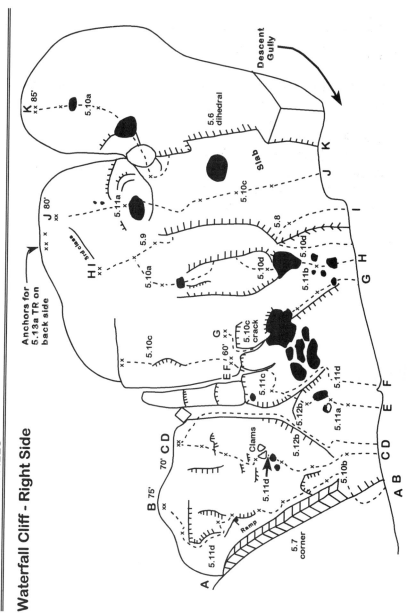

Waterfall Cliff - Left Side

A   **The Falls** 5.8, or 5.10a direct start, pro: small to medium tri-
cams useful in pockets (★★)

B   **The Oracle** 5.11a (★)

C   **The Greeboo** 5.10c (★)

D   **'Charlie Solo' Lieback Exit** 5.6

E   **Anti-Christ** 5.11d, pro: include a medium stopper (★★)

F   **Excessive Force** (Direct start to Anti-Christ) 5.12a (★)

G   **Lieback Corner** 5.7, pro: 1" to 3"

Waterfall Cliff - Left Side

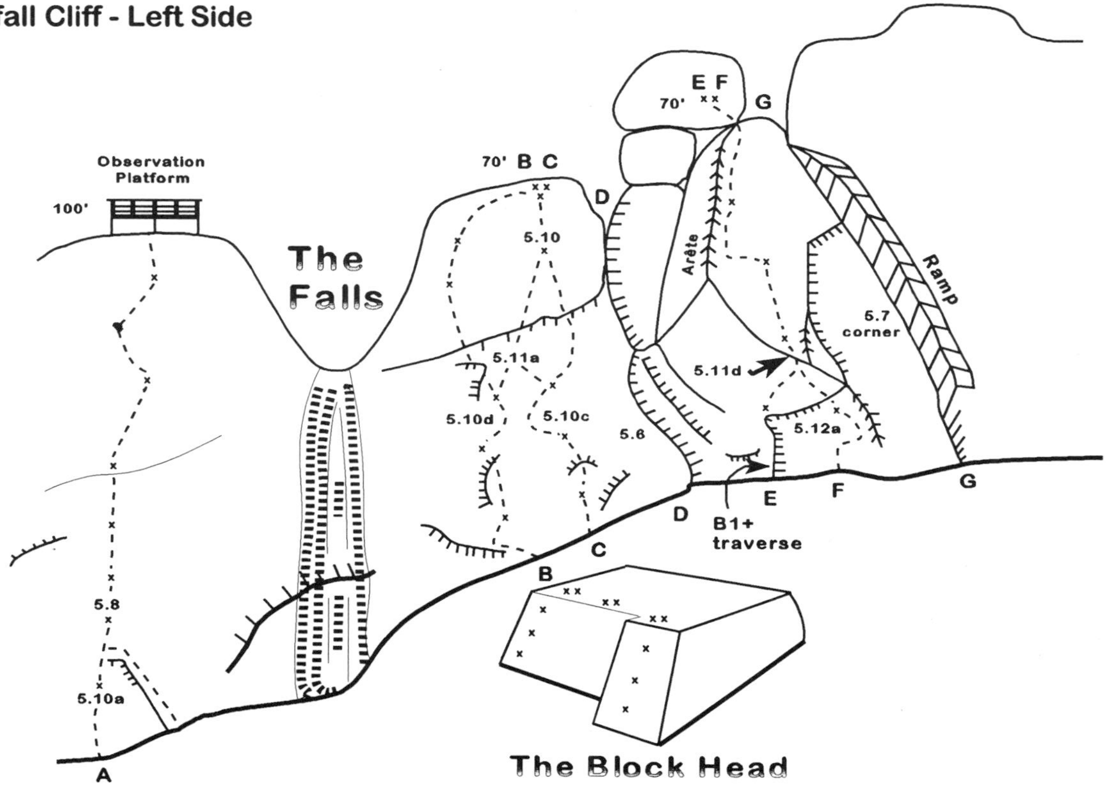

The Falls

The Block Head

Observation Platform

100'

Ramp

5.7 corner

5.12a

5.11d

Arête

B1+ traverse

5.8

E F 70'

70' B C

5.10

5.11a

5.10c

5.10d

5.8

5.10a

A   B   C   D   E   F   G

The Block Head

The Block Head is the large boulder at the base of *Castle Rock Falls*. Although there are only two lead routes, abundant anchors permit multiple top-rope variations.

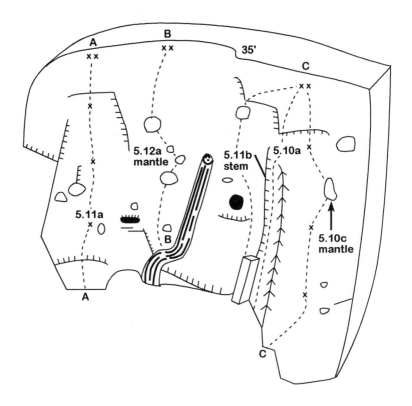

The Block Head

A   **Left** 5.11a R (★)
B   **Center TR** 5.12a mantle
C   **Right** 5.10c (★)

The Slave Cave

This is the poison-oaked infested cave just across the creek to the north of *Castle Rock Falls.*

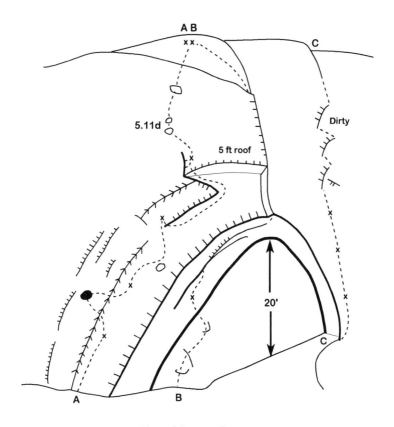

The Slave Cave

A   **Full Of Hatred** 5.11d (★★)
B   **Project - 5.13 Roof**
C   **Old Aid Route**

Chapter 17

LAST TEMPTATION CLIFF

The Last Temptation Cliff is the first major rock formation you will encounter walking the **Ridge Trail** after it splits from the main **Saratoga Gap Trail** to *Castle Rock Falls*. There are several high-quality, moderate routes to enjoy here during the winter months when a southern exposure almost always guarantees shirt-sleeve conditions. During the summer, though, this cliff is best left to the vast local population of rattle snakes.

Left: **Mark Hill on the first ascent of "The Lobotomy" (5.11d), Last Temptation Cliff**

Last Temptation Cliff - Southwest Face

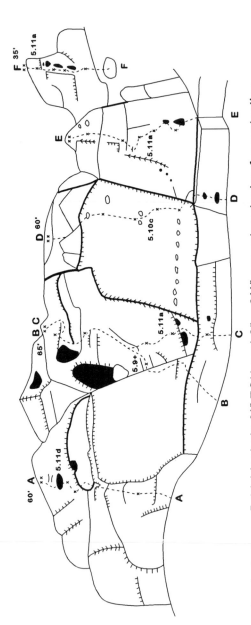

A   **Lobotomy** 5.11d include ¾" TCU and 3" – 3½" camming device for protecting the first and second clips (★)

B   **Chimps In Negligée** 5.9+, pro: ¾" to 2" (★)

C   **Charlie's Angel** 5.11a R

D   **Go I Know Not Wither** 5.10c, pro: include extra ¾" to 2" piece to protect the final roof (★★)

E   **Live Monkey Brain** 5.11a (★★)

F   **Sunset Arête** 5.11a (★)

Chapter 18

GOAT ROCK AREA

Next to **Castle** itself, eighty-foot **Goat Rock** and its smaller next-door neighbor, **Billy Goat**, are probably the two most visited formations in the entire State Park. Popular with novices because of the many accommodating holes and pockets, **Goat** also has a series of large roofs offering harder lines like "Dragon's Breath" (5.11) and the "Lunge." A legendary death-fall bouldering circuit also starts out from the backside of **Goat**. See Chapter 19, pp. 100 - 101 for particulars.

Remember: To prevent further erosion to an environment already badly damaged by pedestrian traffic, the State Park Department requests that you use only designated trails to access the base of Goat Rock.

Billy Goat Rock

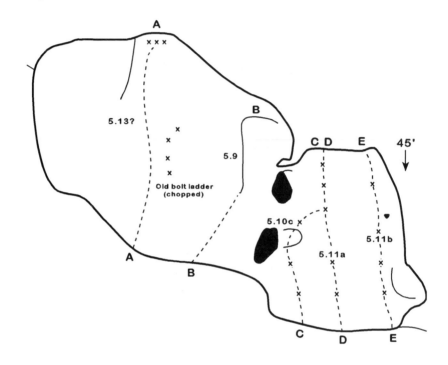

Billy Goat Rock

A   **Face TR** 5.13 (?)
B   **Flake** 5.9
C   **Bridwell Bolt Route** 5.10c (★)
D   **Permanent Erection** 5.11a bulge (★★)
E   **Cummed On** 5.11b/c (★★)

Goat Rock

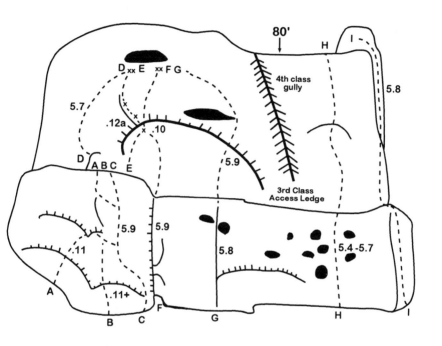

Goat Rock

A	**Dragon's Breath** 5.11 roof lip traverse (★)
B	**Lunge Route** 5.11+
C	**Triple Overhang** 5.9
D	**Overhang Continuation** 5.7
E	**Great Roof- Left Side** 5.12a (★★)
F	**Great Roof** 5.10 (★★)
G	**Center Route** 5.9
H	**Swiss Cheese** 5.4 - 5.7 (★)
I	**Corner Route** 5.8

Butter Buns

Butter Buns lies hidden in tar brush directly below the base of **Goat Rock**. The best way to approach this little orange roof is from below by leaving the the **Saratoga Gap Trail** a couple hundred yards west of the **Observation Platform** at *Castle Rock Falls.*

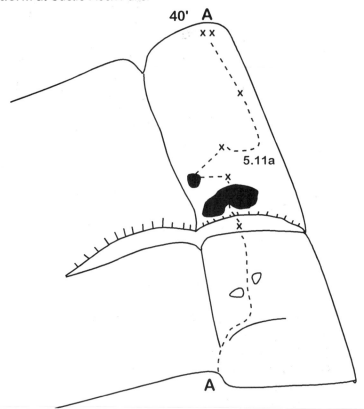

Butter Buns

A   **Center Route** 5.11a roof (★)

Chapter 19

BOULDER PROBLEMS

Long before **Castle Rock State Park** acquired bolted sport routes, the small sandstone outcroppings scattered throughout the madrones, live oaks and bays have offered South Bay climbers challenging high-standard boulder problems and extended circuits similar to those found in the famous enchanted forest at Fountainbleau near Paris. Indeed, some of the best climbing in the whole area can be found on the boulders.

RATINGS

Individual boulder problems are rated according to the Yosemite Decimal System (YDS) up to 5.11d. Above that difficulty, the "B" scale developed by John Gill during the early 1960s is employed.

Some boulder problems are also assigned a spade (♠) rating according to their potential for injury, as follows:

♠ Possibility of lower leg injury (broken ankle, shattered calcaneus, spiral fracture of tibia, etc.)

♠♠ Mandatory physical therapy

♠♠♠ Closed casket funeral

Nature Nazi Boulders

The **Nature Nazis** are a cluster of ten- to twenty-foot boulders in **Sanborn Skyline County Park** just across U.S. 35, a hundred yards east of the main entrance gate to **Castle Rock Parking Lot**. See **Map 4** and **Map 5**.

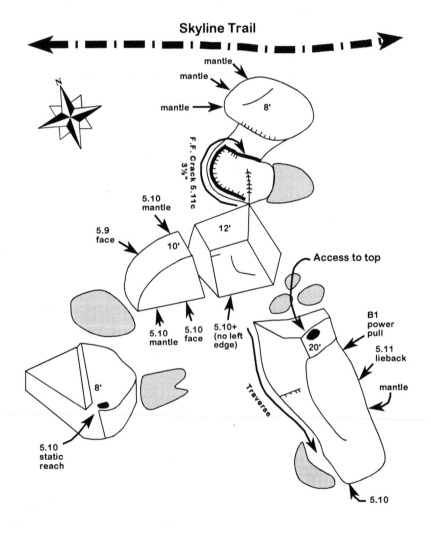

Main Castle Rock Bouldering Areas

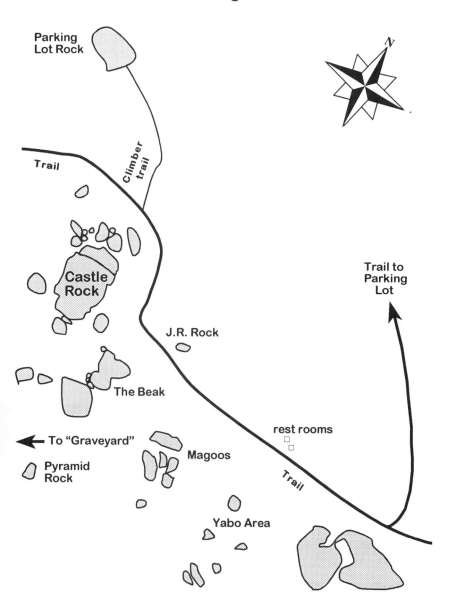

Main Castle Rock

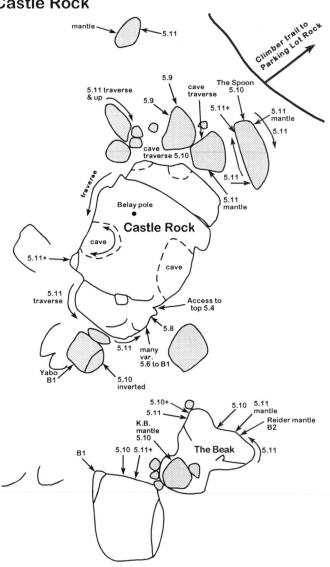

mantle ← 5.11

Climber trail to Parking Lot Rock

5.9

5.11 traverse & up

5.9

cave traverse

The Spoon 5.10

5.11+

5.11 mantle

5.11

cave traverse 5.10

5.11

5.11 mantle

traverse

Belay pole

Castle Rock

cave

5.11+ →

cave

5.11 traverse

Access to top 5.4

5.8

5.11   many var. 5.6 to B1

Yabo B1

5.10 inverted

5.10+
5.11
K.B. mantle 5.10

5.10   5.11 mantle

5.10   Reider mantle B2

B1   5.10 5.11+   **The Beak**   5.11

Magoos and Yabo Area (a.k.a. 'Down Under')

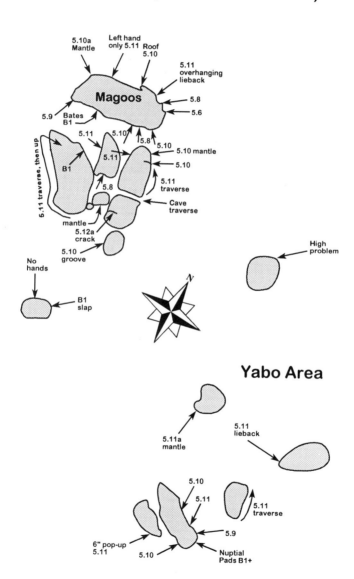

5.10a
Mantle

Left hand
only 5.11

Roof
5.10

5.11
overhanging
lieback

Magoos

5.8

5.6

5.9   Bates
B1

5.11 traverse, then up

5.11

5.10

5.8

B1

5.11

5.8

5.8

5.10

5.10 mantle

5.10

5.11
traverse

Cave
traverse

mantle

5.12a
crack

5.10
groove

No
hands

B1
slap

High
problem

N

Yabo Area

5.11a
mantle

5.11
lieback

5.10

5.11

5.11
traverse

5.9

6" pop-up
5.11

5.10

Nuptial
Pads B1+

Parking Lot Rock

Arguably, one of the best bouldering rocks in Northern California, excluding Yosemite.

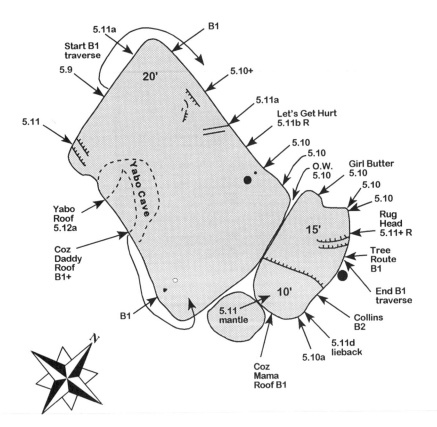

The Graveyard

The Graveyard is situated approximately a hundred yards downhill southwest from the mouth of the giant cave on **Castle Rock**. This area contains three challenging 'pumper' traverses - *"Domino Theory"* (5.11d), *"Egg Head"* (5.11d) and the *"Insecurian Arete"* (5.12a).

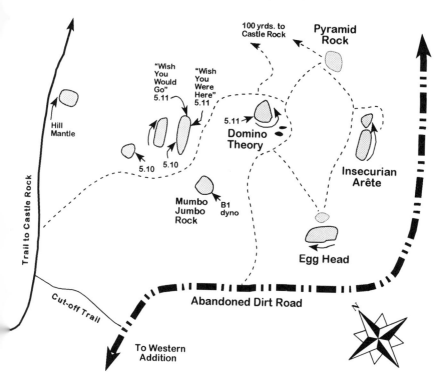

Goat Rock Bouldering Circuit

A difficult bouldering circuit adds excitement to the other top-ropes and leads found on **Billy Goat** and **Goat Rock**. The opposite page shows where to find these demanding problems, many of which were completed during the late 1970's and early 1980s by Scott Cosgrove, David Caunt, Rich Vetter, and Rick Harlan.

1 **Slope Nose** 5.10d
2 **Death & Destruction** 5.11b
3 **Terminator** B1 (♠)
4 **Palm Reader** 5.11a (♠♠)
5 **Grotus Groove** 5.10d
6 **Heinous Rock** 5.11 (♠), three separate problems
7 **Sport Fags** 5.11b
8 **Bottle Rock** 5.11a
9 **Trophy Hunter** 5.11c (♠)
10 **Projectile Vomit** 5.11d
11 **Way Dubious Contortionist** B1
12 **Trail Side Killer** 5.11d
13 **Problem Child** B1+ (♠)
14 **Warm Up** 5.10c
15 **Ball Buster** 5.11a (♠)
16 **Aaron's Mantle** 5.10c
17 **Bowling Bawl** 5.11a
18 **Grand Lizard** B1 (♠)
19 **Devil's Triangle** 5.11b (♠)
20 **Baby Stroller** 5.10-
21 **Jingus Mongoloid** 5.10d (♠)
22 **Kamikaze Arête** 5.11c (♠♠)
23 **Goat Rock Traverse** B1-

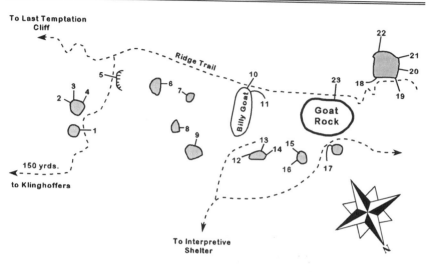

Goat Rock Bouldering Circuit

Klinghoffer Boulders

Each of the three **Klinghoffers** offers exquisite bouldering, often quite high off the ground. Again, the first ascensionists include Cosgrove, Harlan, Vetter and Caunt, sometimes assisted by Eliott Robinson and Kim Dao.

1	**Son of Trail Side** 5.11a
2a	**Oswald Cheese** 5.11b
2b	**Oswald Cheese Direct** B1 (♠)
2c	**Harlan Start** 5.11d
3	**Gray Face** 5.10d
4	**Achielle Larro** 5.11b
5	**Center Crack** 5.10a
6	**Empty Wheelchair** B1
7	**Head Hunter** 5.11a (♠♠)
8	**Abu Nidal Cranks A Rad** 5.11a (♠)
9	**Kim's Death Crack** 5.10c (♠)
10	**Klinghoffer Traverse** (right to left) B1
11	**Lady Di** 5.10d (♠)
12	**Man Overboard** 5.11 c/d (♠)
13	**Pope Drippings** 5.11a
14	**Death Wish** 5.11c (♠♠)
15	**Old Corner** 5.10b
16	**Coz Solo** 5.11c (♠♠♠)
17	**Superman Was Out of Town** 5.11a (♠♠)
18	**Tsunami Arête** 5.11c (♠)
19	**Winnie Mandela Boulder** 5.10

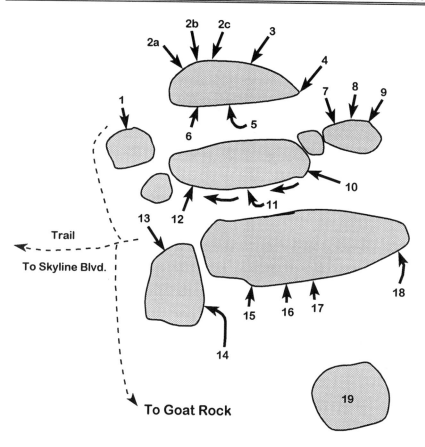

Klinghoffer Boulders

Below: Charles Mulligan on the first ascent of "Charlie's Angel" (5.11a), Last Temptation Cliff

Appendix A

ROUTES LISTED BY DIFFICULTY

All roped lead and top-roped climbs described in this guide are assigned a quality rating, identified by region, and grouped below according to their technical difficulty.

5.4

Summit Route (Castle Rock)

5.6

'Charlie Solo' Lieback Exit (Castle Rock Falls)
Chimney TR (Castle Rock)

5.7

Band Aids On Road Rash (California Ridge - Western Addition)
Hill Solo (Lime Disease Rock)
Lieback Corner (Castle Rock Falls)
Lieback TR (Skyline Slabs)
Overhang Continuation (Goat Rock)
Swiss Cheese (Goat Rock) (★)
U. Santa Clara Practice Climb #2 (Summit Rock)
Wide Crack (Summit Rock)

5.8

Chock Stone TR (Castle Rock)
Chew Tooth - Hand Crack (Western Addition)
Corner Route (Goat Rock)
Slot Nose (Shady Rock - Western Addition)
South Face Route (Indian Rock)
U. Santa Clara Practice Climb #1 (Summit Rock)

5.8 (continued)

Vixen (Lime Disease Rock)

5.9

Balance Sheet (Underworld Rock)
Center Route (Goat Rock)
Chester The Molester TR (Henry & Otis - Underworld)
Chew Tooth - Solo Crack (Western Addition)
Chimps In Negligée (Last Temptation Cliff) (★)
Classic Crack (Eagle Peak) (★)
Claw - Center (Eagle Peak)
Cranberries (Skyline Slabs) (★)
Dirty Mind (Coral Caverns - Aquarian Valley)
Double Cracks (Summit Rock) (★)
Face-Corner (Eagle Peak)
Face TR (Castle Rock) (★)
Flake (Billy Goat Rock)
Hair Dresser (Underworld Rock)
Hand Crack/Roof (Summit Rock)
High On Life (Underworld Rock) (★)
Howling Iguana TR (Platypus - Western Addition)
Ironing Board (Underworld)
Leading To Death (Castle Rock Falls)
Madrone Direct (Green Monster) (★★)
Ribbed For Comfort TR (Summit Rock)
Shit Creek (Stevens Canyon Boulder)
Thin Hands Crack TR (Henry & Otis - Underworld)
Tree Surgeon (Summit Rock) (★)
Triple Overhang (Goat Rock)
Uncle Adolf (Henry & Otis - Underworld)

5.10a

Bitch Goddess TR (Lime Disease Rock)
Blowing Bubbles (Indian Rock) (★)
Case Dismissed (California Ridge)
Cotton Mouth (Shady Rock - Western Addition)
Degeneration (Castle Rock Falls) (★★)

5.10a (continued)

Dog Breath (Shady Rock - Western Addition) (★)
Doughnuts With Buddha (Outriggers - Summit Rock) (★)
Eyes of Love (Tower of Pain) (★)
Falls Direct (Castle Rock Falls) (★★)
Farewell To Arms TR (Castle Rock) (★★)
Flare Up (Outriggers - Summit Rock)
Hit Man (Underworld Rock) (★)
Jelly Belly (Globule - Indian Rock) (★)
Moss Man (Platypus - Western Addition) (★★)
Mud Pies (Mud Wall - Underworld)
Mullah (California Ridge) (★)
Plat-A-Pussy (Platypus - Western Addition) (★)
Puckered Starfish (Indian Rock) (★)
Pyramid Crack (Pyramid Rock) (★)
Rat-A-Puss (Platypus - Western Addition) (★)
Roof TR (Castle Rock - East Face) (★)
Roof TR (Castle Rock - West Face)
Root Canal - flare finish (Summit Rock)
Son of Thoth TR (Gods - Underworld)
Special Effects (Shady Rock - Western Addition) (★)
Suicide Solution (Betty - Aquarian Valley)
Thoth (Gods - Underworld) (★)
Uncle Fred's Vacation Plan (Chew Tooth - Western Addition) (★)
Worm Belly (Summit Rock)

5.10b

Anubis (Gods - Underworld) (★)
Chewy's Lookout (Mother Lode - Devil's Canyon) (★★)
Claw - Left (Eagle Peak)
Great Roof (Goat Rock) (★★)
Green Room (Coral Caverns - Aquarian Valley)
Miles Without Smiles (Tower of Pain) (★★)
Mommy's Boy (Mud Wall - Underworld) (★)
Mud Shark (Mud Wall - Underworld)
Muff Diver (Mid-Muffin - Castle Rock Falls) (★)
Pigs' Feet (Lime Disease Rock) (★★)
Pogo's Nose (Summit Rock)

5.10b (continued)

Psycho Killer TR (Henry & Otis - Underworld)
Shit List (Stevens Canyon Boulder) (★)
Ticks Ripped My Flesh (Lime Disease Rock) (★★)
Twin Oaks TR (Green Monster) (★)
Unnamed (Aquarian Waterfall Wall)

5.10c

Block Head - Right (Castle Rock Falls) (★)
Bridwell Bolt Route (Billy Goat Rock) (★)
Cum Slot (Indian Rock)
Dahmer's Delight (Summit Rock) (★)
Drug Lord (Underworld Rock) (★)
Face (Eagle Peak)
Gestapo Priest (Underworld Rock) (★)
Glob of Shit (Summit Rock)
Go I Know Not Wither (Last Temptation Cliff) (★★)
Greeboo (Castle Rock Falls) (★)
Green Thumb (Coral Caverns - Aquarian Valley)
Mantle Groove TR (Castle Rock)
Mega Blast TR (Castle Rock) (★)
Old Bolt Ladder (Skyline Slabs) (★★)
Peewee's Big Adventure (Summit Rock) (★)
Peewee's Weewee TR (Summit Rock)
Poop Shoot (Underworld Rock) (★★)
POS Crack (Castle Rock Falls)
Roof TR (Green Monster)
Tall Man Simplex (Shady Rock - Western Addition) (★)
Thin Crack TR (Shady Rock - Western Addition)
Vicious Circles (Indian Rock) (★)

5.10d

Al Hussein (Platypus - Western Addition) (★)
Bolt Filcher (Summit Rock) (★★★)
Boogers (Aquarian Waterfall Wall) (★★)
Broken Asshole TR (Gods - Aquarian Valley) (★)
Butt Hole Bypass (Underworld Rock)

5.10d (continued)

Corn Muffin (Lower Muffins - Castle Rock Falls)(★)
Green Bud TR (Mother Lode - Devil's Canyon)
Guilty As Charged (California Ridge) (★)
Happy New Year TR (Sunshine Boulder - Devil's Canyon) (★)
Jelly Roll (Lower Muffins - Castle Rock Falls)
Morris Code (Aquarian Waterfall Wall) (★★)
Morris Minor TR (Aquarian Waterfall Wall)
Pearls Before Swine (Aquarian Valley) (★★)
Small Man Complex (Shady Rock - Western Addition) (★)
Sweaty Eddy TR (Betty - Aquarian Valley)
Tooth & Claw (Stevens Canyon Boulder)
Urolagniac TR (Summit Rock)

5.11a

Access Denied (California Ridge) (★)
Axe Blades From Hell (Skull - Aquarian Valley) (★)
Baby Fat (Globule - Indian Rock) (★★)
Bad Influence (Shady Rock - Western Addition) (★)
Beak (Eagle Peak) (★)
Belly Button (Globule - Indian Rock)
Black Market Babies (Underworld Rock) (★★)
Block Head - Left (Castle Rock Falls) (★)
Brain Food (Devil's Canyon) (★)
Brain Waves (Summit Rock) (★★)
Butter Buns - Center (Goat Rock Area) (★)
Cerberus (Gods - Underworld) (★)
Charlie's Angel (Last Temptation Cliff)
Coral Cavern TR (Aquarian Valley) (★★)
Dragon's Breath (Goat Rock) (★)
Fish On A Tricycle (Stevens Canyon Boulder)
Force Field TR (Stevens Canyon Boulder)
Henry TR (Henry & Otis - Underworld) (★)
Isn't (tree start, Aquarian Waterfall Wall)
Lefthand Arête TR (Underworld Rock)
Light In The Basement (Summit Rock) (★)
Little Shit (Outriggers - Summit Rock)
Live Monkey Brain (Last Temptation Cliff) (★★)

5.11a (continued)

Lucky In Love (Lime Disease Rock) (★)
Mantle TR (Shady Rock)
Molar (Summit Rock) (★★)
Mud Hole (Mud Wall - Underworld) (★★)
Oracle (Castle Rock Falls) (★)
Orange Barrel TR (Orange Sunshine Cliff - Devil's Canyon)
Permanent Erection (Billy Goat Rock) (★★)
Poop Shoot Direct (Underworld Rock)
Putrefaction (Castle Rock Falls) (★★★)
Sahib TR (Summit Rock)
S'not (Aquarian Waterfall Wall) (★)
Sunset Arête (Last Temptation Cliff) (★)
Underpass (Underworld Rock) (★★)
Wanker TR (Ironing Board - Underworld)

5.11b

Aeronautical Engineer TR (Castle Rock) (★★★)
Aquarium TR (Devil's Canyon)
Burnt Muffin (Lower Muffins - Castle Rock Falls) (★★)
California Five-Eleven A (California Ridge) (★★★)
Chew Tooth - Left (Chewtooth - Western Addition)
Convulsions (Castle Rock Falls)(★★)
Cummed On (Billy Goat Rock) (★★)
Face Bitch TR (Coral Caverns - Aquarian Valley) (★)
Fecolagniac (Summit Rock) (★★)
Goin' Down Slow (Vulture - Eagle Peak) (★★)
Hang Nail (Stevens Canyon Boulder)
Hocus (Indian Rock) (★)
Jelly Fish (Platypus - Western Addition) (★★)
La Moulin Rouge (Tower of Pain) (★★)
Mike's Donut TR (Globule - Indian Rock)
Mother Load (Mother Lode - Devil's Canyon) (★★★)
Rectalphobiac (Summit Rock) (★★★)
Unlucky In Love (Lime Disease Rock)
The World Kills Dreamers (Tower of Pain) (★)

5.11c

Caunt Arête (Lime Disease Rock)
Chancroid (Summit Rock)
Dismal Abysmal (Indian Rock) (★)
Donkey Dong (Indian Rock) (★★★)
Effluvia (Stevens Canyon Boulder) (★★)
Embryo TR (Platypus - Western Addition)
Herpes Simplex (Shady Rock) (★)
Little Squirt (Outriggers - Summit) (★★)
Lunge Route (Goat Rock)
Mud Crack (Mud Wall - Underworld) (★)
Otis TR (Gods - Underworld) (★★)

5.11d

Above The Law (Castle Rock Falls) (★★)
Anti-Christ (Castle Rock Falls) (★★)
Ayatollah (California Ridge)
Black Dragon TR (Castle Rock Falls) (★)
Body Cast TR (Mid-Muffin - Castle Rock Falls) (★)
Caunt Arête TR (Tower of Pain)
Chew Tooth - Center (Western Addition) (★★)
Clamydia (Castle Rock Falls) (★★★)
Full of Hatred (Castle Rock Falls) (★★)
Krokus (Indian Rock) (★★★)
Liar's Dice TR (Lower Muffins - Castle Rock Falls)
Lobotomy (Last Temptation Cliff)(★)
Merry Christmas TR (Sunshine Boulder - Devil's Canyon)(★)
Morris Plan TR (Aquarian Waterfall Wall) (★)
Roof TR (Castle Rock)
Skill Saw Gourmet (Summit Rock) (★★★)

5.12a

Block Head - Center TR (Block Head - Castle Rock Falls)
Boogers - Direct Start (Aquarian Waterfall Wall)
Broken Hearts Are For Assholes TR (Asshole - Aquarian Valley) (★)
Cosgrove Face (Lime Disease Rock) (★)

5.12a (continued)

Excessive Force (Castle Rock Falls) (★)
Gold Wall TR (Eagle Peak)
Great Roof - Left Side (Goat Rock) (★★)
Jail Bird, left var. (Indian Rock) (★★)
Man Hole (Tower of Pain) (★★)
Merciless TR (Stevens Canyon Boulder)
Orange Barrel Arête TR (Orange Sunshine Cliff - Devil's Canyon)
Overhanging Seam TR (Castle Rock)
Power Mad TR (ZPG Rock - Devil's Canyon)
Rigormorris (Summit Rock) (★★)
Set (Gods - Underworld)
Stoner Cave TR (Aquarian Waterfall Wall) (★)
Strip Poker (Indian Rock) (★★)
Sweaty Betty TR (Betty - Aquarian Valley) (★★)
TR (Outriggers - Summit Rock)

5.12b

Caunt Face (Aquarian Waterfall Wall)
Cleotitis (Castle Rock Falls) (★★)
Connect The Dots TR (Triangle Rock)
Dentritus TR (Castle Rock Falls)
Fish On A Bicycle TR (Stevens Canyon Boulder)
Give Me Skull TR (Skull - Aquarian Valley) (★)
Jail Bird, right var. (Indian Rock) (★★)
"Los Pistoleros" TR (Tower of Pain)
Panning For Holds TR (Mother Lode - Devil's Canyon)
Skull & Cross-bones (Skull) (★★)
Skull F__k TR (Aquarian Valley) (★)
Snake Pit TR (Vulture - Eagle Peak)
Spung-Lick-A-Litus (Summit Rock) (★★)
Well Endowed TR (Indian Rock)
ZPG Now! TR (ZPG Rock - Devil's Canyon) (★★)

5.12c

Asshole TR (Aquarian Valley)

5.13a

Cave Bitch TR (Coral Caverns - Aquarian Valley)
Goin' Down Fast TR (Vulture - Eagle Peak)
Tidal Wave TR (back side - Waterfall Cliff)

5.13b

Muffin Monster TR (Mid-Muffin - Castle Rock Falls) (★★)

CALIFORNIA
MOUNTAIN
GUIDES

The Bay Area's

Leading

Climbing School

Scott Cosgrove
Owner/Director
Licensed & Insured

For further information call:
(619) 366-3270

ROUTE and CLIFF

INDEX

Yabo Bouldering Area (a.k.a. 'Down Under') (Main Castle Rock Bouldering Areas) 95, 97
Yabo Cave (Parking Lot Rock) 98
"Yabo Roof" B5.12a (Parking Lot Rock) 98

Z

ZPG Rock (Devil's Canyon) 12, 24
ZPG Now! TR 5.12b (Devil's Canyon) 24, 112